D0754570

sustainable CITIES

HOW CAN WE SAVE OUR WORLD?

sustainable

CITIES

Angela Royston

ARCTURUS

This edition first published by Arcturus Publishing
Distributed by Black Rabbit Books
123 South Broad Street
Mankato
Minnesota MN 56001

Printed in the United States

Series concept: Alex Woolf
Editor and picture researcher: Cath Senker
Designer: Phipps Design
Consultant: Howard Sharman, Univerity College London

Library of Congress Cataloging-in-Publication Data

Royston, Angela.
  Sustainable cities / Angela Royston.
      p. cm. -- (How can we save our world?)
  Includes index.
  ISBN 978-1-84837-288-7 (hardcover)
  1. Urban ecology--Juvenile literature. 2. City planning--Environmental
aspects--Juvenile literature. I. Title.

  HT241.R68 2010
  307.76--dc22
                              2009000618

Picture Credits
Chris Fairclough Worldwide: 28 (Edward Parker), 31 (Edward Parker), 33 (John Birdsall),
41 (Chris Fairclough); Corbis: 6 (Jed Leicester/Reuters), 8 (Diego Lezama Orezzoli),
14 (Ciro Fusco/epa), 17 (Smiley N. Pool/Dallas Morning News), 19 (Michael Freeman),
26 (Eric Sierins), 32 (Michael S. Yamashita); EASI-Images (all Rob Bowden except where
indicated) 11 (Simon Scoones), 12, 13, 15, 18, 21 (Miguel Hunt), 25 (Adrian Cooper),
27, 29, 34 (Adrian Cooper), 36, 37 (Neal Cavalier-Smith), 38, 39, 40; Jerry Harrall: 23;
Rex Features: cover; Robert Royston: 43; Science Photo Library (Gary Hincks): 16;
Shutterstock: 7 (Shawn Kashou), 9 (nikolpetr), 30 (Otmar Smit)

Artwork on pages 10, 16 and 22 by Phipps Design

Cover picture
This house in New Mexico is energy self-sufficient, with a wind turbine
and solar water heater.

Credits
Every attempt has been made to clear copyright. Should there be any inadvertent omission
please apply to the publisher for rectification.

CONTENTS

The Pull of the City

Cities all over the world are growing ever bigger: some are so big they merge, creating vast megacities. Cities cover the natural landscape with bricks, concrete, and tar. They suck in huge amounts of resources and spew out enormous amounts of trash. So why do people want to live in cities?

A better life

People come to cities looking for excitement and opportunity. Cities have more colleges, stores, theaters, movie theaters, restaurants, clubs, and music venues than other places. Nevertheless, most people migrate to cities to find work. Cities provide thousands of different jobs, for example, in stores, offices, and factories. Capital cities contain government offices, too. The best-paid and most powerful jobs are usually city-based and draw in well-qualified people from all over the world. Poor people also flock to cities looking for any work they can find.

Many cities have a diverse population. They include people and cultures from many countries. This is the Notting Hill Carnival in London, United Kingdom (UK), a Caribbean festival attended by hundreds of thousands of people.

FACE THE **FACTS**

Tokyo-Yokohama in Japan is the world's largest city by population. More than 34 million people live there. Tokyo-Yokohama is really two cities that have joined to form one. The world's largest city by area is New York. Together with the surrounding towns it has engulfed, the city covers almost 4,300 square miles (11,000 square kilometers).

City needs

More people live in cities than ever before. Just over half the world's population now lives in urban areas, and about half of urban dwellers live in cities of more than 500,000 people. Each large city consumes hundreds of thousands of tons of food, millions of gallons of water, and gigawatts of electricity every day. These are usually brought in from outside. Consumer goods, gasoline, and some foods may even come from the other side of the world.

Are cities sustainable?

Many people are now realizing that cities damage the environment—not just the countryside over which they sprawl but the world environment too. Resources, such as water, food, fuel, and raw materials, are not limitless. City life is unsustainable when the city uses resources faster than they can be replaced. Architects and planners are beginning to think again about how cities operate and how they can be made more sustainable.

Skyscrapers consume vast amounts of building materials, and they are getting taller. Burj Dubai (right), completed in 2009, is about twice the height of the previously tallest buildings, the Petronas Towers in Kuala Lumpur, Malaysia.

CHAPTER 1

Cities in History

Cities became possible only after agriculture was invented about 10,000 years ago in Mesopotamia, in what is now Iraq. By planting crops and herding animals, farmers produced more food than they needed.

Farmers sold their surplus, allowing other people to give up farming and become craftsmen and traders. People lived together in villages and began to rely on each other for the things they needed. Farming and trade spread to other regions, and some villages grew into cities.

Early cities

By 4000 BC, the populations of the largest cities, such as Ur and Sumer, had grown to about 25,000. The most powerful and wealthy people built temples, palaces, and magnificent houses in the center of the city. Poorer people lived around the edge, while outside the city walls were the farmers who grew and sold food to the urban population. Early cities also developed in Egypt, China, and India and later in Greece, Rome, and Central America.

Mohenjo-Daro was built in about 2500 BC in the Indus Valley in what is now Pakistan. It was built on a grid pattern and is the first example of city planning.

Many were built on the banks of rivers, which provided them with water, drainage, and an easy way to move goods in and out by ship.

Medieval cities

Most medieval cities were surrounded by a strong wall. The wall protected the city from attack, but it also limited its size. The wealthiest cities made their money from trade and so were usually built on rivers or on the coast. Goods, made by people in small workshops, were sold locally and sometimes to distant countries. As trade thrived and the population increased, cities spread beyond their walls. The biggest cities, such as Venice in Italy, London in England, and Antwerp in the Netherlands, had several hundred thousand inhabitants.

PERSPECTIVE

Marco Polo (c.1254–1324)

Marco Polo was a great Venetian traveler and one of the first Europeans to visit China. Here he describes the city of Hangzhou:

"The city is beyond dispute the finest and the noblest in the world... And there are in it twelve thousand bridges of stone, for the most part so lofty that a great fleet could pass beneath them... Inside the city there is a lake... and all around it are erected beautiful palaces and mansions, of the richest and most exquisite structure that you can imagine, belonging to the nobles of the city."

As cities became centers of power and wealth, they needed to defend themselves from attack. People in the castle in Carcassonne, France, defended the city.

The staggering rise of cities

The population of cities increased dramatically in the nineteenth century. The expansion began in Britain with the Industrial Revolution, which followed James Watt's invention of the steam engine in 1765. Steam engines were used in mines and factories and to pull trains. This invention was just the first of many new machines that transformed society and cities.

Factories using the new machines produced huge numbers of cheap goods and employed many people. Industrialization soon spread to other European countries and to North America. Towns grew up close to coal mines and quickly grew larger. People moved from the countryside to find work in the factories. They lived in overcrowded slums, in streets that were blackened by smoke from the factory chimneys.

FACE THE **FACTS**

This chart shows the growth of the urban population in each continent since 1950 and the predicted percentage of the population that will live in cities in 2030.

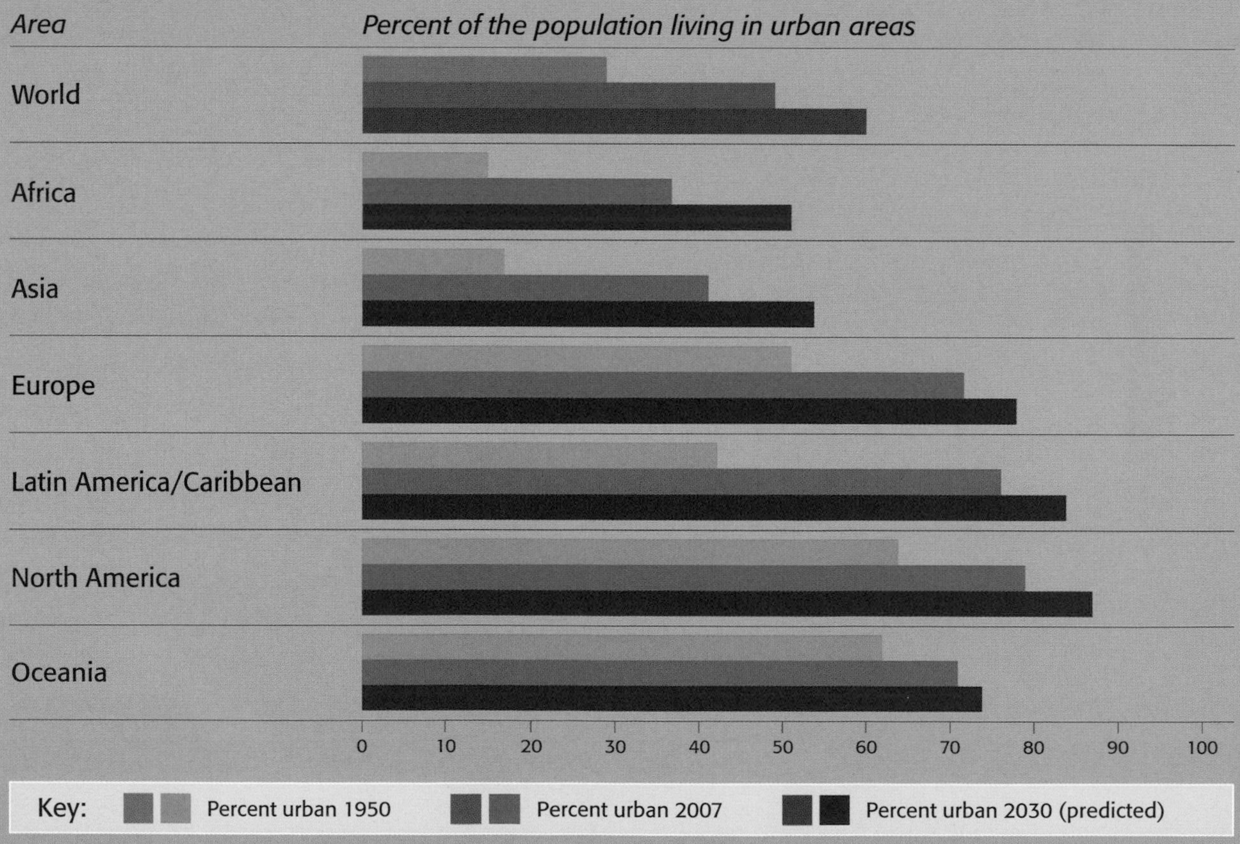

Area — *Percent of the population living in urban areas*

- World
- Africa
- Asia
- Europe
- Latin America/Caribbean
- North America
- Oceania

0 10 20 30 40 50 60 70 80 90 100

Key: Percent urban 1950 · Percent urban 2007 · Percent urban 2030 (predicted)

Source: United Nations, World Urbanization Prospects: The 2005 Revision (2006), and Carl Haub, 2007 World Population Data Sheet.

Gradually, city environments grew better. Factory owners were forced to improve working hours and conditions. An understanding of how germs cause disease led to better sewage systems and safer hospitals. The invention of electricity brought electric lights and machinery. The first oil well, drilled in 1859, led to the invention of the gasoline engine. The earliest cars took to the road in the 1890s, and the first powered aircraft flew in 1904.

Cities in the twentieth century

Oil provided fuel for transport by road, rail, sea, and air. Communications between and within cities increased and became faster. This meant that people could live farther from the city center and commute to work. New materials and building methods transformed city buildings. Skyscraper office blocks now dominate most city centers; they would not have been possible without Elisha Otis's safety elevator and the invention of air conditioning. Cities expanded fast. By 2000, there were 388 cities with more than a million inhabitants, but the United Nations predicts that by 2015, there will be 21 megacities with populations of 10 million or more.

A view toward the ocean from Rochina *favela* (shantytown) in Rio de Janeiro. Much of the urban population growth in poorer countries is in shantytowns.

FACE THE **FACTS**

The fastest-growing cities are in developing countries. In those places, people migrate to cities hoping to find work, better schools and hospitals, and a higher standard of living. In reality, they usually end up in shantytowns on the edge of cities. Shantytowns often have no clean water, sewage systems, or electricity. People build their own homes out of materials such as corrugated iron and cardboard.

CHAPTER 2

Why Cities Are Unsustainable

People need shelter, food and consumer goods, water and power, but most citydwellers have little idea where these supplies come from or what happens to their trash and sewage.

As the population of cities grows, new homes have to be built, using concrete, iron, glass, wood, and other raw materials. Clean water pours from the taps, and dirty water disappears into the drains. Electricity—usually generated in distant power stations—is available at the flick of a switch. It is easy to buy food, clothes, and other goods from city stores. The labels may reveal that the goods have come from China, Brazil, Kenya, or Spain, for example, but they do not tell you how much fuel and resources were used to transport them.

People come from miles around to shop at huge shopping centers, such as this fashionable shopping area in Tokyo, Japan. Most people arrive by car, using fuel and causing pollution. Large areas of land may be paved over to provide parking space for their cars.

PERSPECTIVE

Need or greed?

Indian philosopher and political leader Mahatma Gandhi said, "Earth provides enough to satisfy every man's need, but not every man's greed." World population has tripled since Gandhi's death in 1948, making it ever more urgent that we find ways to provide a good standard of living without draining the earth's resources. Gandhi also said, "Be the change you want to see in the world."

Ecological footprint

Researchers have devised a way of measuring the impact of a city on the environment. It is called its ecological footprint. This is the area of land needed to supply the city and dispose of the garbage. The researchers calculate that the earth has enough resources to sustain an area equivalent to 4.2 acres (1.7 hectares) per person. The current level of consumption, however, is 5.7 acres (2.3 hectares). This means that people are already consuming resources faster than our planet can replace them.

Cities in rich countries have the largest ecological footprints. For example, London relies on an area of land that is 120 times bigger than London itself. This amounts to about 49 million acres (20 million hectares), or about 7 acres (3 hectares) per person. Residents in New York and Boston require even more—20.8 acres (8.4 hectares) of land per person—to maintain their current way of life. This is at least 10 times greater than a similar-size city in India.

A new high-rise building under construction in Tokyo. The huge amounts of raw materials needed to complete the building will be brought in by truck, often from distant factories.

Disposing of waste

A city produces thousands of tons of garbage every day. Garbage cans and dumpsters are emptied regularly. Most garbage is dumped in landfill sites—huge holes dug in the ground on the edge or outside the city. Much of the garbage is made up of plastic and other materials that do not rot but remain in the ground for hundreds of years. Apart from polluting the land, many countries are rapidly running out of space for landfills. Huge incinerators are an alternative to landfills, but burning garbage can produce poisonous gases that pollute the air.

Bags of garbage were piled high in the streets of Naples in Italy after garbage collectors refused to collect it during a dispute in 2008. Problems like this make people aware of the amount of garbage cities produce.

Sewage

Garbage isn't the only waste that people produce. Sewage is carried away in underground pipes, except in most shantytowns, where sewage may run through open ditches. A hygienic sewage system is not the end of the story, however. If sewage is allowed to flow into rivers or the sea, it causes pollution. Sewage plants filter out the waste, clean up the water, and may even turn the remains into fertilizer.

Polluting the air and water

Cities produce tons of waste gases that pollute the air. The gases come mainly from traffic, factories, and power stations. Some of the pollution is invisible, although it may show up as photochemical smog when the sun shines. Other pollution is clearly visible. Many cities are constantly shrouded in haze or, worse still, thick smog. Although pollution may hang over a city, it is also blown by the wind, sometimes hundreds of miles. Lakes and forests in Scandinavia are dying because of rain that has been polluted by smoke and exhaust gases produced by distant cities.

Air pollution is so bad in Tokyo that this bicycle attendant is wearing a mask to filter out harmful gases.

PERSPECTIVE

Face-to-face with sewage

On the Around the World website, Joe Atkins, a sewer worker in New York, recalls when he first started work: "The early days on the job were the hard ones. I remember coming home from work, knocked out from inhaling methane, and falling asleep. I was unprepared for the experience of dealing with raw sewage and rats."

Roger Alva learned to keep his mouth tightly shut in the sewers, but occasionally a splash of filthy water went astray. Then he had to rinse his mouth with a special type of alcohol.

Global warming

There is an even more urgent reason why cities need to become sustainable. The temperature at the surface of the earth is rising. This is called global warming, and although the average rise since 1750 is less than 1.8 degrees Fahrenheit (°F) (1 degree Celsius, °C), it is already dramatically altering weather patterns. Climates are becoming unpredictable, and hurricanes, droughts, and floods are becoming more severe. What is causing global warming?

Greenhouse gases

Greenhouse gases are gases in the air, such as carbon dioxide and methane, that trap the sun's heat, making the earth warmer. We need some greenhouse gases to keep the earth at the right temperature to support the wide variety of life that exists now. The problem is that man-made greenhouse gases are increasing, trapping more of the sun's heat. The main greenhouse gas is carbon dioxide, which is produced when people burn coal, oil, and natural gas. These fuels are called fossil fuels because they formed millions of years ago from the remains of plants and tiny sea animals. As they formed, they locked up carbon. When the fuel is burned, the carbon is released.

About half of the sun's heat is absorbed by the earth's surface. This heat then radiates back into the atmosphere, but greenhouse gases trap and reflect some of it, making the surface of the earth warmer.

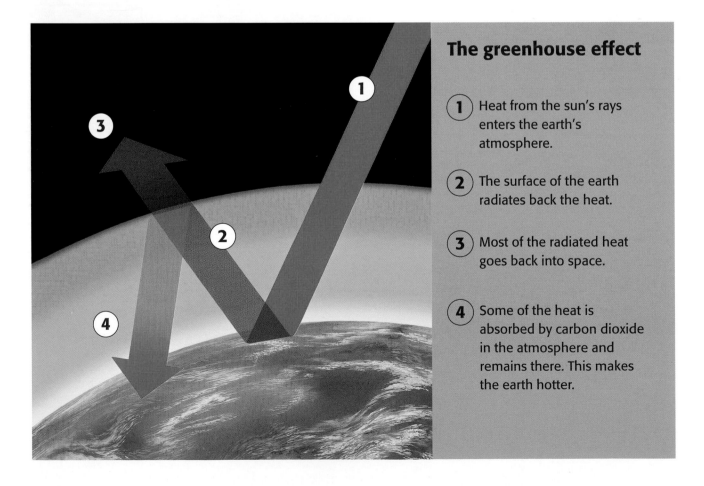

The greenhouse effect

1. Heat from the sun's rays enters the earth's atmosphere.

2. The surface of the earth radiates back the heat.

3. Most of the radiated heat goes back into space.

4. Some of the heat is absorbed by carbon dioxide in the atmosphere and remains there. This makes the earth hotter.

How cities contribute to global warming

Cities burn fossil fuels in many different ways. Road transportation relies on gasoline and diesel, which are both made from oil. The energy to heat and cool buildings is usually generated by burning fossil fuels. Most of the food sold in city stores has been sprayed with pesticides and fertilizers made from oil.

The way ahead

There are ways to make cities more sustainable. Architects need to rethink the way they construct new buildings, in particular which materials they use and where the materials come from. Buildings should be designed so that they use less energy for heating and lighting. Instead of traveling long distances across the city for work, communities can be planned so that more people can work nearer home.

In 2005, New Orleans flooded following Hurricane Katrina. The flood occurred because the city's flood defenses had been poorly maintained. As floods become more common, cities will have to spend an increasing amount of money on flood defenses.

FACE THE **FACTS**

The more the earth warms, the greater the consequences. Scientists predict that an increase of just 3.6°F (2°C) above 1750 levels would, among other things, threaten a quarter of all species with extinction, put 90 to 200 million more people at risk of catching malaria, and make between 226 million and 2 billion more people short of water.

CHAPTER 3

Sustainable Building

In addition to shelter from wind and rain, a building has to provide heating in cold weather and cooling in hot weather. It needs electricity to power computers, lighting, and other devices, and it requires clean water and a system for dealing with garbage and sewage.

Some homes have been built that do all this without producing greenhouse gases or damaging the environment. These "eco-homes" provide blueprints for the future. Eco-homes are built with materials that are found locally and are renewable. Waste and recycled materials satisfy both of these conditions. For example, Earthships are eco-homes designed and built by architect Michael Reynolds in New Mexico. The main building blocks are used tires filled with earth. The tires are stacked up and covered with mud so you cannot see them. Old cans, cardboard, and recycled glass and wood are also used.

The UK's first Earthship was opened in Scotland, in 2004. Built with the assistance of Michael Reynolds, it shows how sustainable building techniques can be adopted in different places.

Some Earthships look bizarre, but sustainable materials can also be used to build more normal-looking homes. They are built with natural materials that are found locally, such as stone and mud. They use wood that comes from managed forests, in which fast-growing trees provide timber and new trees are grown to replace them.

Wonderful mud

Mud is a good building material because it is easily available and insulates against heat and cold. It is used in traditional building methods in many parts of the world. Adobe consists of mud mixed with straw and left in the sun to harden. Mud can also be mixed with cement to make a kind of lightweight concrete. Alternatively, it can be pressed into shape to make thick walls of rammed (compressed) earth.

PERSPECTIVE

Ideal home

Eco-architects claim that eco-homes take advantage of all climates. If it rains, the water is collected. If it is windy, the wind turbine generates electricity. If it is sunny, more electricity is generated. "Imagine a home," Michael Reynolds told *The Independent* newspaper, "that heats itself, that provides its own water, and grows its own food. Imagine that it needs no expensive technology, it recycles its own waste, and it has its own power source. And now imagine that it can be built anywhere, by anyone, out of the things that society throws away."

This traditional building, called a pueblo, in Taos, New Mexico, is made of adobe and blends in with its surroundings. The building has a wood frame made of strong beams that extend beyond the walls. The mud walls are damaged by the weather and have to be replaced from time to time. The wood frame, however, remains.

Generating electricity

Eco-homes produce electricity using wind and sunlight—neither of which will run out. The force of the wind turns the blades of a wind turbine to generate electricity. Wind turbines work best in places that have a steady wind most of the time, such as on the coast or lakeside, on hilltops, or on plains. They work less well in cities, which are usually more sheltered.

Photovoltaic (PV) cells contain silicon crystals that generate electricity from sunlight. The cells are about the same size as roof tiles and usually replace tiles on the side of the roof that catches the most sunlight. PV cells perform best in bright, sunny places, but they also work in cloudy, dim conditions. They do not, of course, work at night. Between them, PV cells and a wind turbine can provide enough electricity to power the lights, computers, and other machines in a home. Once installed, they produce no greenhouse gases.

At present, PV cells are costly to buy. They also have to be kept clean so that sunlight can easily penetrate them. A recent development is to use PV cells in window frames. They are much cheaper and more efficient (see page 31). PV cells work best in hot, sunny countries, but they can also work well in cooler, cloudier countries.

> **SUSTAINABLE TECHNOLOGIES**
>
> # Hydrogen fuel cells
>
> In the future, the most efficient way of generating electricity is likely to be a hydrogen fuel cell. The cell combines hydrogen and oxygen to produce water, electricity, and heat. A fuel cell can work well with PV cells. During the day, excess electricity from the PV cells is used to produce hydrogen from water. At night, the fuel cell uses the hydrogen to generate electricity.

Solar heating

An eco-home is built to take advantage of the sun's heat. Solar water heaters on the roof heat the water. The building has large windows that face the sun to take in heat on cool days. This is called passive solar heating. With good design and insulation (see page 22), very little extra heat is needed in winter, but a wood-burning stove can be used if necessary. Trees or awnings shelter the same windows in summer, when the aim is to keep the inside cool.

Heat pumps

Heat pumps make use of a difference in temperature between two places, either inside and outside a building or the temperature at ground level compared with several yards underground. A heat pump transfers heat from one place—usually the warmer place—to the cooler place. The system works best when the difference in temperature is not too large.

Solar cells can be used on existing buildings as well as on new buildings. The dark panels on the walls of this block of apartments in Berlin, Germany, are PV cells that generate electricity.

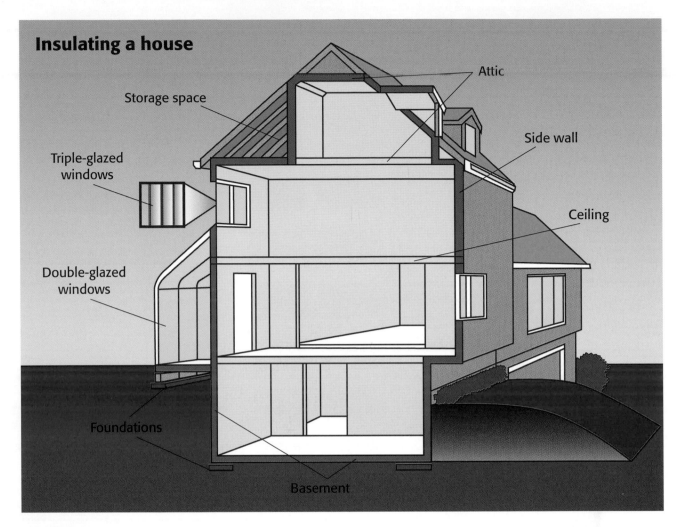

Insulating a house

Storage space

Attic

Triple-glazed windows

Side wall

Double-glazed windows

Ceiling

Foundations

Basement

Insulation

Insulation keeps a building warm in winter and cool in summer. Some eco-homes use earth and plants to insulate the building from the outside. This mimics the burrows of animals, such as rabbits and gerbils, which survive extreme heat or cold by living underground. Traditional thatch also insulates the roof. A more conventional way to insulate a building is to put insulating material between the top floor and the roof and on the outer wall of the building. However, many insulating materials are synthetic, which means that many of them are made from oil. Homes that are completely carbon free use a natural material, such as sheep's wool.

Double glazing and draft proofing

Windows let in light, but they also allow heat to escape. Double-glazed windows lose much less heat because they have two panes of glass with air, or better still argon gas, between them. Triple-glazed windows have three panes of glass and lose even less heat. Warm air also escapes around windows and doors unless

The best way to insulate a house is to cocoon it by laying insulating material under the ground floor, on all of the outside walls, and in the attic. Double or triple glazing insulates the windows. In this diagram, the layers of insulation are shown in pink.

the gaps are sealed with foam or brushes. This is called draft proofing. Insulation, double glazing, and draft proofing can save 30 percent of the energy used to heat a building.

Natural ventilation

Instead of having air conditioning in summer, new homes can be designed to be cool and use natural ventilation. Many of the techniques are copied from traditional buildings in hot countries. In these places, homes are often built around a shady courtyard and have few windows on the outside walls. Wind catchers are based on a traditional idea but have been adapted to modern buildings. A wind catcher is a double vent in the roof. Hot air from the building rises and escapes through one vent while fresh, cool air is drawn down the other vent to replace it.

PERSPECTIVE

The Hobbit house

Jerry Harrall built an earth shelter for his family in Lincolnshire, UK. He told *The Guardian* newspaper, "Occasionally we get called Hobbits, but we're not underground—we're in a bungalow covered in earth. I think we've created an environment of serenity and tranquillity. One side faces south with a lot of glass, so we have a high level of daylight. The rest, including the roof, is covered in earth planted with ivy, which reduces the rate of heat loss and acts as sound proofing. Although we have no heating, the temperature remains between 64 and 70°F (18 and 21°C)."

Jerry Harrall's earth shelter is built of heavyweight material that stores heat. The outside is covered with a type of polystyrene that acts as a super-insulator.

Reducing demand for water

In many cities, water is in short supply. As a city grows larger, its demand for water increases, but the supply may not be able to keep pace. Some cities, such as Melbourne in Australia, are also suffering from increasing drought owing to climate change. Water is wasted too. In most countries, tap water is filtered and cleaned so that it is safe to drink. Yet most of this costly clean water is used in toilets and flushed down the drains! Cities need to use much less water.

Saving water

Eco-home owners save water in several ways. They collect rainwater in a water tank and recycle bathwater, washing machine water, and other "gray" water. In some eco-homes, this water is filtered several times so that it is safe to drink, but most people simply use gray water for flushing toilets and watering the garden. Other ways of saving water are also encouraged, such as having a shower or a smaller bath. Toilets, dishwashers, and washing machines are chosen to use as little water and as little energy as possible.

SUSTAINABLE TECHNOLOGIES

Compost toilet

One of the simplest ways to deal with sewage is to have a compost toilet. There are many different designs available, but the purpose of all of them is to turn human sewage into compost that can be used to enrich the soil. Dry-composting toilets do not use water and so are useful in areas that often have droughts. The technology for composting toilets is improving, so that the smell is reduced and less space is needed to compost the sewage. Compost toilets are particularly useful in places that are not connected to the sewage system.

Closer to nature

Most sustainable housing includes a garden or shared gardens. These provide a space that usually includes trees and a pond or running water. Some have roof gardens as well as ground-level gardens. Studies have shown that people benefit from being in touch with nature. It relieves stress and keeps them in touch with the changing seasons.

Gardens are also used for growing food. Many eco-home owners are able to grow most of the vegetables they need and some of the fruit. Turning sewage into compost provides free fertilizer and allows them to produce organic food, grown without artificial chemicals.

This roof garden on top of a building in Beijing, China, provides a peaceful escape from the busy streets below. Its plants may also help to soak up some of the city's pollution and improve the air quality.

CHAPTER 4

Eco-communities

Cities in many different countries have built eco-communities. For example, Freiburg, Germany, has a sustainable community of 5,000 homes. Australia's Olympic Village, originally built for the 2000 Olympic Games in Sydney, has been developed into a green suburb with many sustainable features.

Some countries plan to build whole new eco-towns, but many people think that these plans are too ambitious. In 2008, for example, Britain's plan to build up to 10 new eco-towns, each housing about 30,000 people, was cut down to just two towns. China has the biggest plan of all—for Dongtan, a city for 1 million people, powered entirely by renewable energy. Whatever their size, eco-communities use many of the same ideas as eco-homes, but the planners have to find ways of making transportation and other systems sustainable too.

The Olympic Village in Sydney is now an eco-community. The buildings face the midday sun so they benefit from passive solar heating in winter. Awnings shade the windows in summer.

Hammarby Sjöstad is a large eco-community that is being built on a brownfield site in Stockholm in Sweden. When it is completed in 2010, it will provide apartments and work spaces for about 30,000 people on land that was once used for docks and industry.

Generating extra electricity

Photovoltaic cells and rooftop wind turbines may not provide enough electricity for an entire community. A combined heat and power (CHP) station is an efficient way of generating electricity locally. In a conventional power station, much of the energy available in the fuel is lost as heat. In a CHP station, the waste heat is used to heat water that is piped into local buildings for central heating. Some CHP stations burn natural gas, which produces less carbon dioxide than burning coal or oil. In an eco-town, the CHP station may burn wood chips or organic farm waste.

Transportation links

Eco-towns and communities aim to reduce car travel, both within the town and from the community to the rest of the city. To achieve this, they have to be situated close to fast rail or bus links into the city center and to other parts of the city.

When allocating housing, many eco-communities give priority to those who do not own cars. Instead, they encourage residents to walk or bicycle by providing bicycle routes and safe, pleasant walking routes around the community.

Working close to home

Many suburbs and commuter towns become like ghost towns during the day because most of the residents travel to work elsewhere. In the past, it was healthier and safer to build homes well away from factories that belched out smoke and poisonous gases. However, many countries today have far fewer factories, so it is not always necessary to separate work and home. Eco-communities are increasingly including offices and other workplaces within their schemes. Working close to home not only cuts down on traveling but also makes the community livelier during the day. Parents can spend more time with their children and be more flexible about the hours they work.

This bank in Heidelberg, Germany, has large solar panels on the roof that generate electricity for use inside the building.

Sustainable buildings

It is difficult to make large buildings totally carbon free, but it is possible to design sustainable buildings using a mixture of low-tech and high-tech features. For example, a building can be designed to use as much natural daylight as possible and so save electricity. Computers can monitor the temperature and lighting in each room and adjust them so that they are kept comfortable without wasting electricity. Some buildings use innovative ways of saving energy. A nightclub in London, for example, has special crystals in the floor that produce electricity when people dance on them!

Computers that have LCD monitors use 77 percent less energy than older monitors. They are also more comfortable to work with because they have less glare and emit less radiation.

SUSTAINABLE TECHNOLOGIES

Eco-city council offices

In 2006, the Melbourne City Council opened a new 10-story council building called Council House 2 (or CH2). It was designed to save energy and water. The building uses fresh air instead of air conditioning. It has photovoltaic cells and six wind turbines to generate electricity. It also has a micro-turbine to generate extra electricity to heat water for the building. Rainwater is collected, and waste water is recycled. These and other features mean that CH2 uses only 30 percent of the water and 15 percent of the energy of a conventional office building.

CHAPTER 5

Making Existing Cities Greener

The problems of climate change and decreasing supplies of resources are so immediate that we cannot wait for new buildings to gradually make cities sustainable. Cities also have to reduce the amount of energy and resources that existing buildings use.

The owners of this old house have placed photovoltaic cells over the roof to generate electricity.

To achieve this, national, state, and local governments and city residents need to work together. Local governments could take the lead, setting targets and giving advice. They should also give money to people who cannot afford to pay for the necessary changes themselves.

Adapting buildings

Luckily, many of the devices and techniques used in eco-buildings also work in conventional buildings. Solar water heaters and photovoltaic cells can both be added to existing roofs. The most suitable roofs are those that face toward the midday sun. On flat roofs, the panels and cells are tilted to catch the most sunshine. In some places, extra electricity made by PV cells is bought by an electricity company and fed into the national grid.

This building, which is being constructed from wood and natural materials, is right in the center of Berlin. Office buildings are constantly being pulled down and redeveloped. This gives an opportunity for the new buildings to be designed to be sustainable.

Saving energy

The easiest way to save energy is to cut out waste—most people waste about a third of the energy they use. For example, traditional incandescent lightbulbs burn five times as much electricity as compact fluorescent lightbulbs (CFLs). A staggering 90 percent of the electricity that traditional bulbs use is wasted as heat. CFL bulbs also last about eight times as long. Since fewer are needed, this means that less greenhouse gas is created by the production of lightbulbs.

Governments can help speed up the change to CFL bulbs by banning the sale of traditional bulbs. In 2005, for example, Cuba changed all of its lightbulbs to energy-saving ones. The Australian government announced in 2007 that the sale of traditional lightbulbs would be banned by 2010.

Insulation

Insulation that is used in new buildings can be added to older buildings. The insulation can be glued to the outside walls. However, since about the 1920s, most homes have been built with cavity walls, which means that the outer wall consists of two walls with a space between them. Cavity walls are better insulators than single-thickness walls, and filling the cavity with insulating foam makes them better still. Insulation can be added to existing attics, and windows can be draftproofed and double glazed. Although insulation costs money, it also saves money by reducing heating bills.

SUSTAINABLE
TECHNOLOGIES

Efficient photovoltaic cells

Photovoltaic cells are expensive to produce and buy, but scientists at the Massachusetts Institute of Technology (MIT) have devised a way to reduce the size of the PV cells and use them on windows instead of roofs. The glass windowpanes are coated with a transparent dye that collects sunlight and directs it to the cells, which are in the window frame. The technique means that each cell can produce 10 times more electricity than those used on roofs.

Sustainable food

Stores and residents can both play their part in reducing the amount of fuel used to bring food into the city. The farther away the food comes from, the more fuel is burned in transporting it. Flying in fresh food from distant countries by aircraft produces many tons of greenhouse gases.

City dwellers can help by buying locally grown food. Many stores in Britain, for example, label food to show where it comes from. Some include an airplane logo on food that has been flown in. Farmers' markets are increasingly popular in many countries. Instead of selling their produce to stores and supermarkets, some farmers take it to markets in local towns and cities. The farmers get a better price for their products, and the customers can buy fresh food directly from the people who grew it.

Growing your own

The best way to eat fresh, local food is to grow your own! Wherever people live, it is usually possible to grow tomatoes, herbs, and vegetables in plant pots and window boxes. People with gardens can grow more vegetables. In Britain, cities are required to put land aside for allotments—small individual plots of land for growing fruit and vegetables. Recently, allotments have become so popular that there are often long waiting lists for them.

This outdoor farmers' market, selling fresh carrots and celery, looks as if it is in a small market town, but it is actually in Union Square in the middle of New York!

An allotment holder (opposite) plants lettuces in the Rotonda de Cojimar allotment garden, in Havana, Cuba.

PERSPECTIVE

Enjoying the freshest food

The fresher food is, the better it tastes. This is what one allotment holder says: "Once you've tasted 'allotment snacks' such as strawberries two seconds off their stems and exploding with taste or raw peas sweeter than sweets, you are spoiled for life. This is 'no-food-miles food' grown in soil that you have dug yourself. It doesn't get better than that!"

Changing planning laws

In the past, many local governments planned cities so that some areas were mainly for homes and others for industry and commerce. It makes sense to keep oil refineries, chemical factories, and any site that is noisy or produces unhealthy or dangerous substances away from residential areas. However, most offices are safe and clean. Where feasible, planning laws could be changed so that more people can work closer to home and so save time and fuel commuting across the city.

Recycling

Most cities are beginning to tackle the problems of waste by recycling as much of it as possible. Paper, glass, tin cans, and some plastic bottles can all be recycled. Food scraps and garden waste can be made into compost. Local government sets up the system for collecting garbage and sorting it, but people need to use the system. Some local governments require people to put their trash into separate bins, depending on the material. Kamikatsu, a village in southwestern Japan, has a zero waste policy, which means that all of its rubbish is recycled. To achieve this, residents have to sort their garbage into 34 different bins!

FACE THE **FACTS**

Recycling a ton of paper saves:

- 7,800 gallons (30,000 liters) of water
- About 3,500 kilowatt hours of electricity

Recycling a ton of steel saves:

- 1.6 tons (1.5 metric tons) of iron ore
- 40 percent of the water used to make new steel
- 75 percent of the energy used to make new steel

Processing recycled materials

Most materials that are recycled are processed and used again. Once metal cans reach the recycling center, for example, they are separated into steel and aluminum. They are then melted down and rolled into thin sheets of metal, ready to be used again. It can take just 60 days for a drink's can to be made into a new can that is filled, sold, and recycled again. Recycling uses some energy, but it takes much less energy to make paper, glass, and metal from recycled materials than it does from raw material.

Plastic

Plastic is the most difficult material to recycle because there are several different kinds. In theory, most types of plastic can be recycled, but this means sorting out each kind and recycling it separately. In practice, it is usually only plastic milk and drink containers that are recycled.

This worker in Beijing, China (opposite), is sorting out plastic garbage that can be recycled.

CHAPTER 6

Getting Around the City

Transportation is the lifeblood of a city. Vehicles move people, goods, and materials from place to place and in and out of the city. Cars, motorcycles, bicycles, buses, and streetcars compete for space with trucks and vans. The result is heavy air pollution and often traffic congestion.

The way to make cities more sustainable is to reduce the amount of traffic, especially private cars. Yet many city governments are more concerned about controlling the traffic and keeping it flowing.

Roads

Newer cities, such as Los Angeles and Singapore in China, have been built to accommodate private cars. Multi-lane highways cross the city, and shopping malls have large parking areas. Many older cities have copied this policy. Roads have been widened and flyovers built to speed traffic in and out of the city. Ring roads around and within the city help traffic to avoid the city center. However, fast roads built to relieve congestion

Although Seoul, South Korea, has many multi-lane highways to ease the flow of traffic, there is still congestion.

often attract extra vehicles and quickly become congested too. Fast roads also create pollution and noise, and because they are difficult and unpleasant to cross, they divide communities.

Speed controls

One way to keep traffic moving is to control the speed at which it flows. Speed cameras monitor the traffic and help to identify places where congestion is building up. In quiet, residential streets, traffic is slowed down by building humps in the road or making the road narrower in places. This is called "traffic calming" and it reduces accidents.

Discouraging cars

The richer the city, the more cars it has. City streets in poorer countries, such as India and Indonesia, are busy but less congested because fewer people own private cars. They travel by motorcycle or bicycle instead. Rather than trying to rebuild cities to accommodate cars, many older cities are now trying to discourage people from using their cars except when essential.

SUSTAINABLE TECHNOLOGIES

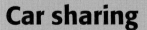

Car sharing

London is one city where car-sharing schemes are growing fast. Instead of owning their own car, people who join the scheme have access to a pool of cars, which they book and pay for by the hour. The scheme works best for people who can switch to using public transportation and only need a car occasionally.

Bicycles are cheap, carbon free to ride, and very versatile. This trader on the island of Java in Indonesia is transporting several cages of birds on his bicycle.

Parking restrictions

The easiest way to dissuade people from using their cars in a city is to make parking difficult and more expensive. Parking may be limited to garages and to parking spaces on the street that have to be paid for. Instead of putting money into a parking meter, the latest schemes allow drivers to pay for parking by credit card using their cell phones. In some places, residents have to buy a special permit to park in the street outside their home. This prevents non-residents from parking there.

Car-free zones

Some cities have gone even further—they have banned cars from the city center. City centers are usually the oldest part of a city. The streets are often narrow

Shoppers and tourists stroll along pedestrianized streets in the center of Barcelona, Spain.

and easily become clogged with traffic. Some cities have reclaimed parts of their city centers for pedestrians by making whole streets and areas car free to allow people to wander safely and freely.

Congestion charging

Many cities are too large to keep cars out of the entire city center. London was the first city to try a new plan—every car that drives into the center has to pay a daily congestion charge. Instead of driving in by car, people are encouraged to use public transportation and to cycle or walk.

Bicycle paths

Cycling is healthy and produces no greenhouse gases or pollution. Cycling in a city can be dangerous, however, particularly along fast roads. City governments can encourage people to cycle by planning bicycle routes and making bicycle paths. These paths are signposted routes that avoid the busiest roads. Bicycle paths are designed to separate bicycles from the rest of the traffic. In some cities, the path is a section of the road marked off by white lines. Even better are the bicycle paths in cities such as Copenhagen, which are separate from both roads and pavements.

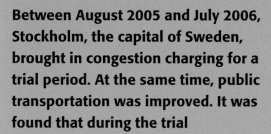

FACE THE **FACTS**

Between August 2005 and July 2006, Stockholm, the capital of Sweden, brought in congestion charging for a trial period. At the same time, public transportation was improved. It was found that during the trial

- **Rush hour traffic was reduced by 20 to 25 percent**
- **Time spent lining up in traffic jams was reduced by 30 to 50 percent**
- **Air pollution was reduced by 14 percent.**

Bicycle taxis, such as this one in Tokyo, are common in many countries in Asia. They are now being used in cities in Europe and North America too.

Improving public transportation

The key to persuading people to leave their cars at home is a fast, reliable, and cheap public transportation system. Public transportation—buses, streetcars, and trains—declined as the number of cars in cities increased. If cities are to become more sustainable, local and national governments need to spend money to improve these services.

Buses

Buses have the huge advantage that they run on existing streets and roads. The challenge is to help them avoid traffic jams and run regularly and reliably. One way to do this is to create special bus lanes. A bus lane is a section of the road that is reserved for buses and often taxis and bicyclists too. In many cities, buses are linked to a GPS navigation system, which informs passengers waiting at bus stops when the next bus is due.

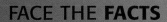

FACE THE **FACTS**

Most US cities are dominated by cars, but Portland, Oregon, has one of the best public transportation systems in the world. One Portland family accepted a challenge to give up their SUV for a month and travel only by public transport. They were so surprised at how easy it was to get around the city using the light railway, buses, streetcars, bicycle lanes, and free city center transportation that they decided to sell their SUV!

London is famous for its red double-decker buses—bus routes crisscross the city. Bus lanes and a pre-pay fare system have greatly helped to speed up traveling by bus.

Streetcars

Streetcars, powered by overhead electric cables, also use the streets but run on special rails. In the past, many cities had cheap streetcar services, but the rails were pulled up because they got in the way of cars. In recent years, many cities have set up new streetcar services. They cause less air pollution than buses, but they are only truly sustainable if the electricity they use is generated without producing greenhouse gases.

Trains

Trains are the fastest form of public transportation. Many cities have underground as well as aboveground trains. Some cities, for example, in Germany, have railway systems that run above the street on elevated tracks. Most railway lines were built to run from the edge of the city into the center. Now cities need to add new lines so that people can move across the city too.

Modern streetcars speed past road traffic in Barcelona, Spain. Planners in the city realized that they could set up a streetcar system more cheaply and quickly than an underground rail system.

CHAPTER 7

Better for Everyone

Making cities more sustainable is good for everyone. Sustainable cities benefit the world by consuming fewer resources and producing fewer greenhouse gases. They benefit residents because they are healthier and less stressful places to live.

These cities put people in touch with the wider environment by making them more aware of the materials and energy they use. Trees, plants, and green spaces play an essential part by providing a direct link with the natural world.

Importance of trees

Many city streets are lined with trees and shrubs. During daylight hours, their green leaves take in carbon dioxide from the air and release oxygen, making the air cleaner and healthier to breathe. In summer, they shade the pavements and the buildings. They soften the hard edges and surfaces of streets and buildings, bringing a reminder of the natural world. Street trees can be cut back from time to time so that they do not take up too much space and to prevent their roots from damaging buildings.

SUSTAINABLE TECHNOLOGIES

A pleasant working environment

The ING Bank building in Amsterdam was designed to save energy and provide the best-possible working environment for its employees. It includes art, natural materials, and water features. The building is surrounded by gardens with running water, and every worker sits within 23 feet (7 meters) of a window. Mirrors in the ceilings reflect the daylight to make the rooms even brighter.

Parks and gardens

Parks are invaluable to city dwellers. They are quiet and peaceful places away from the bustle and noise of the streets, where people can walk or simply sit and think. They provide space for jogging, playing catch, and many other healthy activities. Parks have enough space to allow trees to grow to their full height, providing food for birds, squirrels, and many kinds of insects. In summer, they create shade for people.

Lakes and waterways

Many parks and public gardens include lakes or large ponds. They attract ducks and other waterfowl. Many cities are rediscovering old waterways—streams, rivers, and canals—which were once used to transport goods. Opening up the paths alongside waterways creates interesting and unusual nature walks—a sliver of countryside through the middle of a city.

Singapore has a treetop walk through natural rain forest on high ground in the middle of the city. The 6-mile (10-km) walk gives views of the city below and of birds, monkeys, and other wildlife in the trees.

argon A colorless gas that does not react with other substances.

commuter town A town where most of the residents travel to nearby cities to work.

compact fluorescent lightbulb (CFL) An energy-saving lightbulb that produces light when electricity is passed through a gas, making it glow.

compost The rotten remains of plants and living things that can be used as a fertilizer.

congestion Overcrowding on the roads, which causes traffic jams.

consumer goods Goods, such as televisions, washing machines, and clothes, that make life more comfortable.

developing countries Poorer countries, where a smaller percentage of people work in factories and offices than in richer countries.

drought A prolonged period with little or no rain.

eco-home A home that produces few or no greenhouse gases and less damage to the environment than other homes.

ecological footprint A measure of the area of land needed to provide each person with everything he or she consumes and to dispose of the waste produced.

fertilizer Substances added to the soil to feed plants and make them grow better.

filtered Passed through charcoal, sand, or other substances in order to remove impurities.

gigawatt A measure of electricity equal to a million watts.

GPS navigation system A way of tracking vehicles using a global positioning satellite. A receiver on the vehicle is linked to a control room via the satellite.

greenhouse gases Gases in the atmosphere that trap the sun's heat.

gray water Water that is not clean enough to drink but is clean enough for other purposes, such as watering the garden.

hurricane A tropical storm that begins over the ocean and develops spiraling winds of more than 74 miles (120 km) per hour and heavy rain.

hydrogen fuel cell A device that generates electricity by combining hydrogen with oxygen.

incinerator A furnace that reduces garbage and other things to ash.

Industrial Revolution A period in history between about 1750 and 1850 when industry developed rapidly and goods began to be made in large quantities in factories.

insulate To prevent the movement of heat from one place to another.

landfill System of disposing of garbage by burying it in the earth.

malaria A disease spread by infected mosquitoes.

methane A greenhouse gas that traps 20 times as much heat as carbon dioxide, weight for weight. It is an efficient fuel and is the main ingredient of natural gas.

pesticide A chemical used to kill pests on crops and livestock.

photochemical smog Smog produced by the action of sunlight on pollution.

photovoltaic (PV) cell A device that changes sunlight into electricity.

raw material A substance in its natural state, such as wood, mineral ores, and oil, that is used to make goods.

recycling Processing unwanted materials so that they can be used again.

renewable Able to be renewed. Wind and sunlight, for example, are renewable sources of energy because they will not run out.

resource A supply of something, such as crops, coal, and water, that can be used to satisfy a need.

shantytown Unofficial settlement that people build near or in a city.

slum An area of a city that is very poor and where the houses are in bad condition.

solar water heater A device that uses the heat of the sun to heat water.

suburb An area of a city that is outside the city center.

sustainable Able to keep going. A sustainable city does not use resources faster than they can be replaced or renewed.

sustainable energy Energy that comes from sustainable or renewable sources, such as wind and the power of the sun.

SUV (sports utility vehicle) A large, powerful car that can be driven off-road.

thatch Roofing material made from straw, reeds, or other plants.

unsustainable Using resources faster than they can be replaced or renewed.

ventilation Replacement of used air with fresh air.

wholesaler A person who buys goods in large quantities and sells them on in small quantities.

wind turbine A device for generating electricity using the power of the wind.

BOOKS

Bowden, Roy. *Sustainable World: Cities*. KidHaven Press, 2004.

Orme, Helen. *Earth in Danger: Climate Change*. Bearport Publishing, 2008.

Rodger, Ellen. *Building a Green Community*. Crabtree Publishing, 2008.

Royston, Angela. *Eco-Action: Buildings of the Future*. Heinemann Library, 2008.

Woodward, John. *Eyewitness: Climate Change*. Dorling Kindersley, 2008.

WEBSITES

http://geography.about.com/library/weekly/aa011201g.htm
Gives statistics on the largest cities over the last 5,000 years.

http://science.nasa.gov/headlines/y2002/solarcells.htm
NASA website: how photovoltaic cells work.

http://www.energysavingtrust.org.uk
Explore this website to find out how homes can be improved to save energy and how they can generate their own electricity.

http://www.epa.gov/climatechange/
United States Environmental Protection Agency website on climate change.

http://www.greenhomebuilding.com/earthship.htm
All about the different materials that are used to build Earthships.

http://www.greenpeace.org.uk/efficiencity/about
Efficiencity is a virtual sustainable town created on the Greenpeace website. Click for an interactive visit to the town to see how it works.

http://www.prb.org/Articles/2007/623Urbanization.aspx
Looks at increasing urbanization of the world's population and the effect of cities on the environment.

http://www.wasteonline.org.uk/index.aspx
Gives information and statistics about savings made by recycling different materials.

INDEX

Page numbers in **BOLD** refer to illustrations.